Stefan Is a Sculptor

by Christine Losq
illustrated by
Stephen Costanza

Harcourt

Orlando   Boston   Dallas   Chicago   San Diego

Visit *The Learning Site!*
www.harcourtschool.com

Stefan Saal is a sculptor.
When Stefan was small, his
family had a cabinet.

Stefan liked to look at the
carvings on the cabinet.
When Stefan grew up, he
became a sculptor.

Stefan carves wood. A sculptor works hard. The work is not quick.

4

One day, Stefan was carving
big chunks of wood. A girl and
her family came by to watch
him.

"This work is not quick," the
girl said.

"A sculptor can't quit until the
work is done," said Stefan.

6

"How do you get ideas for your work?" the girl asked.

"I like to read," said Stefan.

"I like to read books about stars and planets. I like to read books about shapes."

"What is this work about?" the
girl asked. Stefan grinned.
"What do you see?" he asked.

"I see a family," said the girl.
"This is about a family," said
Stefan. "Which one do you like
best?"

"What does this writing say?"
a boy asked. Stefan helped the
boy read the writing on his
sculpture.

When Stefan goes home, he
sees the cabinet. He still likes
the carvings as much as he
did when he was a boy.